I0415793

May 2012

2020 CENSUS

Additional Steps Are Needed to Build on Early Planning

GAO

Accountability ★ Integrity ★ Reliability

GAO
Accountability * Integrity * Reliability

Highlights

Highlights of GAO-12-626, a report to congressional requesters

2020 CENSUS

Additional Steps Are Needed to Build on Early Planning

Why GAO Did This Study

GAO's prior work has shown that it will be important for the Bureau to reexamine its management and culture as well as the fundamental design of the census in order to ensure a cost-effective census. The Bureau recognizes this and has taken steps in at least three management areas toward achieving these goals. As requested, this report addresses the extent to which the Bureau is taking steps in accordance with selected leading practices that GAO identified for (1) organizational transformation, (2) long-term project planning, and (3) strategic workforce planning in preparing for the 2020 Census. To meet these objectives, GAO identified leading practices in these areas that are relevant to the Bureau's 2020 Census planning, reviewed Bureau documents, and interviewed officials.

What GAO Recommends

GAO recommends that the Census Director take a number of actions to make 2020 Census planning more consistent with key practices in the three management areas, such as examining planned transformation activity to ensure its alignment with resources, developing a more-detailed long-term schedule to smooth transition to later planning phases, implementing effective congressional outreach to ensure a stable planning environment, and setting workforce planning goals and monitor them to ensure their attainment.

The Department of Commerce concurred with GAO's findings and recommendations and provided minor clarifications, which were included in the final report.

View GAO-12-626. For more information, contact Robert Goldenkoff at (202) 512-2757 or goldenkoffr@gao.gov.

What GAO Found

The Census Bureau's (Bureau) early planning and preparation efforts for the 2020 Census are consistent with most leading practices in each of the three management areas GAO reviewed. For example, with respect to its effort to transform its decennial organization, top Bureau leadership has been driving the transformation, and the agency has focused on a key set of principles as it begins to roll-out the strategy to staff. Furthermore, the Bureau has created a timeline to build momentum and show progress. At the same time, however, the amount of change-related activity the Bureau is considering as part of its reorganization of its decennial directorate may not be aligned with the resources the Bureau has allocated to plan, coordinate, and carry it out, and, as a result, the planned transformation efforts may not be sustainable or successful.

Similarly, the Bureau is taking steps consistent with many of the leading practices for long-term project planning, such as by, among other activities, issuing its series of 2020 planning memorandums in 2009 and 2010 that laid out a high-level framework documenting goals, assumptions, and timing of the remaining four phases of the 2020 Census. The Bureau also created a high-level schedule of program management activities for the remaining phases, documented key elements such as the Bureau's decennial mission, vision, and guiding principles, and produced a business plan to support budget requests, which is being updated annually. Still, the Bureau's schedule does not include milestones or deadlines for key decisions needed to support transition between the planning phases, which could result in later downstream planning activity not being based on evidence from such sources as early research and testing. Furthermore, there has been little effective outreach to the Bureau's congressional stakeholders about its reexamination of census processes and design, which could result in a lack of support on potentially complex or sensitive topics that can be crucial for creating a stable environment in which to prepare for a census.

In the area of strategic workforce planning, the Bureau is taking steps consistent with leading practices such as by identifying current and future critical occupations with a pilot assessment of the skills and competencies of selected information technology 2020 Census positions. However, the Bureau has done little yet either to identify the goals that should guide workforce planning or to determine how to monitor, report, and evaluate its progress toward achieving them, which could help the Bureau identify and avoid possible barriers to implementing its workforce plans.

The steps the Bureau has taken and has planned are positioning it well during this early phase of planning for the 2020 Census. Since much of the Bureau's early progress is tied to additional planning and other activity needed over the coming months, equally important will be the need to execute these activities in a timely manner to maintain the Bureau's early momentum toward a cost-effective 2020 Census.

Contents

Table

Figures

Abbreviations

Bureau	U.S. Census Bureau
HCAAF	Human Capital Assessment and Accountability Framework
IT	Information Technology
OIG	Office of Inspector General

United States Government Accountability Office
Washington, DC 20548

May 17, 2012

Congressional Requesters

The characteristics of the census—long-term, large-scale, complex, high-risk, and politically sensitive—together make a cost-effective enumeration of the nation's population and housing a monumental project-planning and management challenge. In preparing for the 2020 Census, the U.S. Census Bureau (Bureau) faces the daunting task of successfully counting a population that is growing steadily larger, more diverse, and increasingly difficult to enumerate in an environment of rapidly changing technology. Challenges in managing and planning the 2000 and 2010 Censuses led to acquisition problems, cost overruns, and other issues, and, as a result, we placed both enumerations on our High-Risk List.[1] Furthermore, the 2010 Census was, at about $13 billion, the costliest U.S. Census in history.

Our work on prior censuses has shown that it will be important for the Bureau to reexamine both the fundamental design of the enumeration, as well as its management and culture to ensure that the Bureau's business practices and systems enable the Bureau to reach its goal of a cost-effective census.[2] And our work has shown that, as a part of robust early planning for the decennial, applying leading practices for planning long-term complex projects from the very beginning can help reduce cost and risk.[3] Consistent with this, the Bureau has stated that to contain costs and maintain quality, bold innovations in both planning and design of the 2020 Census will be required. For example, in fiscal year 2011, the Bureau completed the initial stage of a transformation effort intended, in part, to fundamentally overhaul the Bureau's approach to planning the decennial

---

[1]GAO, High-Risk Series: Quick Reference Guide, GAO/HR-97-2 (Washington, D.C.: February 1997) and 2010 Census: Automation Problems and Uncertain Costs and Plans May Jeopardize the Success of the Decennial and Warrant Immediate Attention, GAO-08-550T (Washington, D.C.: Mar. 5, 2008).

[2]GAO, 2010 Census: Data Collection Operations Were Generally Completed as Planned, but Long-standing Challenges Suggest Need for Fundamental Reforms, GAO-11-193 (Washington, D.C.: Dec. 14, 2010).

[3]GAO, Decennial Census: Additional Actions Could Improve the Census Bureau's Ability to Control Costs for the 2020 Census, GAO-12-80 (Washington, D.C.: Jan. 24, 2012).

GAO-12-626 2020 Census Early Planning

census. The Bureau created a new 2020 Census Directorate and a 2020 Research and Planning Office to take the lead for 2020 preparations. Furthermore, during the past year the Bureau began a process of identifying the skills gap in its workforce in order to have the skills and competencies it needs for developing a more cost-effective 2020 Census. As the Bureau continues planning the 2020 Census, it will be important that it implement leading management practices in each of these areas.[4]

Instilling leading management practices will also be important for sustaining the Bureau's transformation efforts and bringing about lasting reforms, especially given the turnover that has been occurring at the head of the agency over the last 40 years. As we noted in our April 2011 testimony, leadership continuity is critical to sustain efforts that foster change, produce results, mitigate risks, and control costs over the long term.[5] However, since 1969 only one Census Director has served longer than 5 years, and the rest—including the current director who recently announced plans to resign from the Bureau in August 2012—served an average term of about 3 years.

In this context, we were asked to assess the extent to which the Bureau's 2020 Census Directorate and its 2020 Research and Planning Office are taking steps consistent with leading practices for (1) organizational transformation, (2) long-term project planning, and (3) strategic workforce planning for the 2020 Census.

To meet these objectives, we reviewed existing leading practices for organizational transformation, long-term project planning, and workforce planning that we and other organizations have previously developed, and identified those that are most relevant to the Bureau's early planning for the 2020 Census. We also reviewed Bureau documents and interviewed Bureau officials involved in the early planning for the 2020 Census. Using these sources, we assessed the extent to which the Bureau was implementing the leading practices. More information on our scope and methodology can be found in app. I.

---

[4]Another management area where the Bureau will need to focus its planning efforts is the area of information technology. We have ongoing work in this area and plan to issue a report on this issue later this year.

[5]GAO, *2010 Census: Preliminary Lessons Learned Highlight the Need for Fundamental Reforms*, GAO-11-496T (Washington, D.C., Apr. 6, 2011).

We conducted this performance audit from August 2011 through May 2012 in accordance with generally accepted government auditing standards. Those standards require that we plan and perform the audits to obtain sufficient, appropriate evidence to provide a reasonable basis for our findings and conclusions based on our audit objective. We believe that the evidence obtained provides a reasonable basis for our findings and conclusions based on our audit objective.

Background

The Bureau's experience with the 2010 and prior enumerations has shown that lack of proper planning and not following leading practices in key management areas can increase the costs and risks of later downstream operations. Leading up to the 2010 Census, we reported on internal organizational, planning, funding, and human capital challenges that jeopardized the Bureau's overall readiness. For example, we reported that additional costs and risks associated with the data capture technologies used in the 2010 Census were related to a failure to adequately link specifications for key information technology (IT) systems to requirements.[6] And the lack of skilled cost estimators for the 2010 Census led to unreliable life-cycle cost estimates. Some of the operational problems that occurred during the 2010 and prior censuses are symptomatic of deeper organizational issues. For example, a Bureau self-assessment carried out in October 2008 found that its organizational structure made overseeing a large program difficult and hampered accountability, succession planning, and staff development.

We and other organizations, including the Bureau itself, have stated that fundamental changes to the design, implementation, and management of the census must be made in order to address these and other problems.[7] In addition, the Bureau Director has testified that various parts of the Bureau could collaborate more effectively. In response, the Bureau has started numerous change initiatives, some directed at transforming the Bureau's organization itself in addition to reexamining its fundamental approach to how it will conduct the 2020 Census.

---

[6]GAO, *Information Technology: Census Bureau Needs to Improve Its Risk Management of Decennial Systems*, GAO-08-79 (Washington, D.C.: Oct. 5, 2007).

[7]GAO, *2010 Census: Preliminary Lessons Learned Highlight the Need for Fundamental Reforms*, GAO-11-496T (Washington, D.C.: Apr. 6, 2011).

The Bureau's organizational transformation took a significant step forward in July 2011 when it created a 2020 Census Directorate, with decennial planning being led by its 2020 Research and Planning Office. The Bureau is targeting to complete further reorganization of its decennial units by the end of fiscal year 2013. In order to obtain necessary approval from the Department of Commerce, the Bureau has set a target of February 2013 for submitting a proposal to the department. To support the organizational transformation effort, the Bureau has designated an "organizational change manager," responsible for planning and managing the day-to-day organizational change activities. Relatedly, the Bureau is attempting to develop Bureau-wide, or "enterprise," standards, guidance, or tools, in areas such as risk management, project management, systems engineering, and IT investment management in order to reduce duplicative efforts across the Bureau.

The Bureau is also reexamining how it fundamentally conducts the decennial census, committing to identify and implement innovation and improvements as necessary to conduct the 2020 Census at a lower cost per housing unit than the approximately $100 per housing unit cost of the 2010 Census (in constant 2010 dollars) while still maintaining high quality. To do so, the Bureau has divided the 14-year life cycle of the 2020 Census into five phases, beginning in fiscal year 2009 with Options Analysis. The figure below illustrates the sequencing of the five 2020 Census phases. The current, second, phase, Early Research and Testing, comprises 35 research projects that are intended to explore how design areas could be modified to control costs or improve quality, such as by using the Internet, social media, and administrative records.[8]

---

[8]We are separately reviewing specific design elements the Bureau is researching, and expect to issue a report later in the year.

Figure 1: The Life Cycle of the 2020 Census Has Five Phases

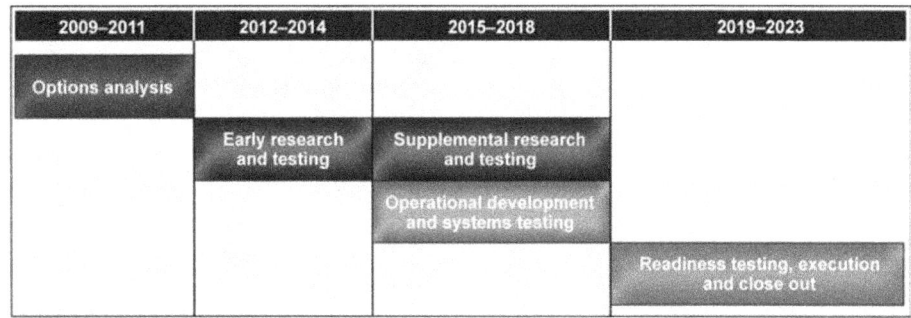

2009–2011	2012–2014	2015–2018	2019–2023
Options analysis			
	Early research and testing	Supplemental research and testing	
		Operational development and systems testing	
			Readiness testing, execution and close out

Source: U.S. Census Bureau.

As the Bureau reexamines how it will plan the 2020 Census, it is also reviewing the employee skills and competencies needed to make that happen, in part by a formal analysis comparing its needs to its in-house capabilities being carried out by its Human Resources Division in collaboration with the 2020 Census Directorate. One of the Bureau's objectives listed within its early planning documents is to have a highly competent workforce that is matched with the demands of the 2020 Census. The Bureau's 2008 internal assessment found that some activities involving the management of large programs and projects, cost estimation, and IT lacked staff with core skills and experience. The Bureau has said that it needs to develop a clear understanding of how existing skill sets align with emerging needs, determine the best use of resources to close competency gaps, and provide information to employees and managers to guide continuing workforce development.

The Bureau Is Beginning an Organizational Transformation Using Key Practices, but Further Planning Is Needed

The Bureau is undertaking an organizational transformation of its entire decennial directorate in order to improve collaboration and communication across its divisions, improve operational efficiencies, and instill a culture that, according to the Bureau, encourages risk-taking and innovation without fear of reprisal. The Bureau believes such change is necessary so that it can more-effectively control costs and enumerate the population for 2020. In 2010, the Bureau generally completed its peak census data-collection activities consistent with its operational plans and released the state population counts used to apportion Congress on December 21, 2010, several days ahead of the legally mandated end-of-year deadline, but did so at a cost that was higher than originally estimated. The Bureau is incorporating several leading organizational transformation practices, which we have previously reported can help individuals affected by the organizational change adapt to the new organization, while simultaneously managing the risk of reduced productivity and effectiveness that often occurs as a result of change. Our prior work has identified key practices in effective organizational transformation, six of which are[9]

- ensure top leadership drives the transformation,
- focus on a key set of principles and priorities at the outset of the transformation,
- set implementation goals and a timeline to build momentum and show progress,
- dedicate an implementation team to manage the transformation process,
- involve employees to obtain their ideas and gain ownership for the transformation, and
- establish a communication strategy to create shared expectations and report related progress.

The Bureau is at an early stage of planning for its transformation, and has a difficult road ahead to finish the planning and begin implementing it. As shown in figure 2, the Bureau has taken numerous steps consistent with the key practices. For example, the Bureau Director has **led the drive for the reorganization,** speaking in public and to Bureau staff a number of times about the need for the Bureau to change if it is to remain cost-effective and relevant in the 21st century. Following the announcement of the Director's upcoming August 2012 departure, several Bureau executives said that they remained committed to the initiatives and vision shared by the Director, including the organizational transformation. In addition, the Bureau has **focused on a key set of principles and priorities at the outset of the transformation**, by including in its change-strategy documents not only explicit reliance on the guiding principles for the 2020 Census, but specific principles to guide the transformation itself, such as "make data-driven decisions," "be responsive and transparent to decennial staff and stakeholders," and "focus on an efficient and resilient organization." The Bureau has also created a high-level transformation **timeline to build momentum and**

---

[9]GAO, *Results-Oriented Cultures: Implementation Steps to Assist Mergers and Organizational Transformations,* GAO-03-669 (Washington, D.C.: July 2, 2003). We previously identified nine leading practices, but selected six as most appropriate for the Bureau at this time.

show progress that includes milestones such as staff workshops and deliverables such as multiyear roadmaps.

Figure 2: Bureau Is Using Selected Key Practices to Carry Out Organizational Transformation for 2020 Census Directorate

Directions:

 Roll over each **Extent consistent** bar to see more information regarding illustrative steps taken and illustrative steps remaining that contributed to the rating given.

Ensure top leadership drives the transformation

- Define and articulate a compelling reason for change.
- Document rationale, expected benefits, and definition of success.

Generally consistent

Focus on a key set of principles and priorities at the outset of the transformation

Embed core values in every aspect of the organization to reinforce the new culture.

Generally consistent

Set implementation goals and a timeline to build momentum and show progress

- Make public implementation goals and timeline.
- Monitor employee attitudes and take appropriate action.

Generally consistent

Dedicate an implementation team to manage the transformation process

- Establish networks to support implementation team.
- Select high-performing team members.

Partially consistent

Involve employees to obtain their ideas and gain their ownership for the transformation

- Use employee teams.
- Incorporate employee feedback.
- Delegate authority to appropriate organizational levels.

Generally consistent

Establish a communication strategy to create shared expectations and report related progress

- Communicate early and often.
- Ensure message consistency.
- Encourage two-way communication.
- Provide information to meet employee needs.

Generally consistent

Source: GAO analysis of U.S. Census Bureau information.

Notes:

Illustrative steps taken to date: GAO assessments based on Bureau steps taken as of April 10, 2012.

Extent consistent: We determined that steps taken or planned were either *"generally," "partially," or "not"* consistent with respective practices.

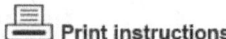 **Print instructions** | To print text version of this graphic, go to appendix II.

Figure 2 also shows that the Bureau plans to take further steps over the next year. For example, the Bureau is planning to roll out much of its transformation planning to its staff in June 2012. In July, the Bureau plans to more directly engage decennial staff by beginning a series of data-collection activities, intended for staff to identify which decennial planning processes work well and which need improving, and is considering reliance on focus groups, online staff surveys, or workshops. Eventually, and subject to sustained progress of the transformation process, the Bureau plans by February 2013 to propose specific changes to its decennial organization and finalize a timeline for carrying out the transition to a new organization, subject to approval of the changes by the department and the Office of Management and Budget.

Although the Bureau is taking and planning many positive steps toward carrying out its organizational transformation, it may be falling short in its **use of an implementation team**. Specifically, the amount of change-related activity being planned may not be aligned with the resources the Bureau has allocated to plan, coordinate, and carry them out. While Bureau organizational transformation documents were largely in draft and subject to change at the time we completed our review, the multiple workshops being planned, the preparation of multiple plan and strategy documents referenced as deliverables, as well as the collation and analysis of data to be collected from staff, seem to be substantial work for the sole staff member dedicated at this time to the transformation. That person, the current organizational change manager, has time divided among transformation planning and implementation, support of the executive council advising on the transformation, leading a working group on decennial strategic workforce planning, and leading a working group on 2020 Census organizational change management communication as well. We have previously observed that a strong and stable implementation team responsible for the transformation's day-to-day management is important to ensuring that transformation receives the focused attention needed to be sustained and successful. If activity planned for the transformation is not aligned with the resources dedicated to it, various change initiatives may not be sequenced or implemented in a coherent and integrated way, collected data may not be properly analyzed and used, and risks to implementation may not be identified or properly mitigated.

In written comments on our draft report, the Department of Commerce responded that after receiving the draft the Bureau assigned additional staff and a contractor to support the Bureau's organizational transformation activity. This action appears responsive to our finding, and, as follow-up to this report, we will assess any action the Bureau may take to examine the alignment between the levels of activity planned for the transformation and the resources dedicated to their implementation.

A More Detailed Schedule Could Improve the Bureau's Existing Project Planning Framework

The Bureau is incorporating several long-term project-planning practices that—if continued and built upon throughout the decade—should help the Bureau avoid many of the management problems it has experienced in prior censuses. For example, the Bureau experienced cost overruns for the 2010 Census in large part because it had to abandon expensive plans for increased use of automation in its field operations late in the planning cycle. Furthermore, preparing a rigorous long-term project plan will help the Bureau demonstrate to Congress and other stakeholders that it can effectively design and manage operations as well as control costs. Our prior work has identified key practices for effective long-term project planning, five of which are[10]

- develop a project plan,
- involve stakeholders,
- incorporate lessons learned,
- analyze and mitigate risks, and
- monitor progress.

As shown in figure 3, the Bureau is taking steps to plan the 2020 Census generally consistent with two of the five key practices we identified and partially consistent with the other three. For example, early on, from June 2009 to November 2010, the Bureau began the practice to **develop a project plan** by issuing a series of eight 2020 planning memorandums[11] that laid out a framework documenting goals, assumptions, and timing of the remaining four phases of 2020 Census. The Bureau also created a high-level schedule of program management activities for the remaining four phases, documented key elements such as the Bureau's decennial mission, vision, and six guiding principles, and produced a business plan to support budget requests, which is being updated annually. Also,

---

[10]GAO, *2010 Census: Cost and Design Issues Need to Be Addressed Soon*, GAO-04-37 (Washington, D.C.: Jan, 15, 2004). We separate "involve stakeholders" and "incorporate lessons learned" here, and exclude "evaluate human resource implications" since we address human capital practices more extensively elsewhere in the report.

[11]U.S. Census Bureau, 2020 Census Information Memoranda Series, Memorandum No. 1-8 (June 22, 2009–Nov. 16, 2010).

consistent with this practice, the Bureau has identified 19 specific management-process areas from management literature and other sources, for which it is developing strategies and plans, such as for knowledge management and performance management (a complete list is included in app. V).

The Bureau also took steps to **involve stakeholders** internally in its early planning when it officially kicked off the 2020 Census on October 3, 2008, with a summit of decennial-census managers discussing challenges, strengths, and weaknesses that would inform the 2020 Census strategic decision-making process. The Bureau began briefing external stakeholders in 2009, describing its approach and high-level plans for the 2020 Census at professional-association meetings, at meetings at the National Academies of Sciences, and to oversight groups such as the Department of Commerce Office of Inspector General (OIG) and us. To help implement the practice to **incorporate lessons learned**, in 2011 the Bureau created a recommendation follow-up process, built around a database it created containing recommendations made in recent GAO and OIG reports on the 2010 Census, and the Bureau has begun including recommendations from its own 2010 Census evaluation reports as well. Not having a formal process for recommendation follow-up for prior censuses made it difficult to ensure that recommendations were systematically considered by those at the Bureau best able to act on them. In concert with a knowledge-management strategy, the Bureau has provided these recommendations to relevant Bureau research and testing teams for their consideration.

Figure 3: Bureau Has Developed a High-Level Framework Generally Using Key Leading Practices for Planning Long-Term Complex Projects

Directions:

 Roll over each **Extent consistent** bar to see more information regarding illustrative steps taken and illustrative steps remaining that contributed to the rating given.

Develop a project plan

Consider all phases of the project and have clear and measurable goals; clearly state all assumptions, schedules, and deadlines; and identify needed skills and resources.

Partially consistent

Involve stakeholders

- Involve internal and external stakeholders in the decision-making process.
- Focus on the highest-priority stakeholder needs and mission goals.

Partially consistent

Incorporate lessons learned

- Evaluate past performance and capitalize on lessons learned to improve performance.
- Include the processes required to use project information to improve future efforts.

Partially consistent

Analyze and mitigate risks

- Identify, analyze, prioritize, and document risks. Ideally, assess more than one alternative.
- Plan risk management—the process of defining how to conduct risk management activities for a project.

Generally consistent

Monitor progress

Identify measurable performance goals that describe and guide successful planning. Collect performance data and report it to determine how well the goals are being achieved.

Generally consistent

Source: GAO analysis of U.S. Census Bureau information.

Notes:

Illustrative steps taken to date: GAO assessments based on Bureau steps taken as of April 10, 2012.

Extent consistent: We determined that steps taken or planned were either "*generally,*" "*partially,*" or "*not*" consistent with respective practices.

 **Print instructions** | To print text version of this graphic, go to appendix III.

Figure 3 also shows that the Bureau plans to take further steps over the next several months. For example, the Bureau is planning in August 2012 to finalize both the detailed schedule of all program management, systems engineering, and training activities for the current research and testing phase of the 2020 Census, as well as all of the individual project plans for the research and testing projects that it began during fiscal year 2012. According to Bureau officials, these processes will evolve and mature as the Bureau learns from the initial implementation and progress from one phase to the next. And in September, it will issue its initial plan for managing communications on 2020 Census planning, progress, and design with established 2020 Census external advisory boards as well as its own staff.

While the Bureau is taking steps generally consistent with two of the five leading practices we identified in this area, additional steps are needed to better implement three practices presented in figure 3. For example, to better **develop a project plan** for long-term projects having multiple phases, the Bureau can take steps to address three weaknesses with its current scheduling. First, it will be important for the Bureau to include milestones marking deadlines and decisions that affect later phases. The Bureau's business plan for the 2020 Census notes one lesson it is trying to leverage from prior censuses is to ensure that evidence from such sources as research and testing is used to inform later planning. But, current Bureau plans provide inadequate detail on when key decisions will need to be made to support transition between the planning phases. For example, while the Bureau has research and testing activity continuing until 2018, it is not clear what specific activity must be completed to inform design decisions that need to be made before the next phase—operational development and systems testing—begins. With the next phase scheduled to begin as early as 2015, if the needed activities are not completed on time, the Bureau is at risk of not starting downstream operations on schedule.

Second, Bureau planning documents do not yet specify when milestones for management activity will—or needs to—transition from the earlier research and testing phase to later phases of 2020 Census planning. Documentation of Bureau management planning focuses naturally and primarily on the current research and testing phase, and much of it states explicitly that the scope of consideration is limited to the research and testing phase. Bureau officials explained that they expect to update most if not all management plans for later phases according to experience gained with them during early research and testing as well as the special needs of later phases. Yet without a schedule for concerted planning to create, revise, or update management plans to address the needs and circumstances of later phases beyond research and testing, the Bureau may find itself in transition without the management plans ready. This runs the risk of the Bureau having to develop and manage parallel processes if new ones need to be created before it has taken steps to decide how pre-existing ones should be revised to support later phases. A more-visible reflection of projected deadlines, or milestones, for decisions related to later phases can help ensure that all necessary efforts leading up to those milestones are prioritized and completed on schedule.

Third, the Bureau is still unsure when some initiatives to implement Bureau-wide, or "enterprise," solutions in a variety of management areas will be completed. The enterprise solutions the Bureau is implementing show promise to reduce duplication of effort and improve consistency by introducing common standards, processes, tools, and systems in areas such as risk management, project management, systems engineering, and IT investment management.[12] Yet robust planning relies on integrated scheduling to ensure that related and dependent activities are coordinated and sequenced properly. Uncertainty over when enterprise solutions that 2020 Census is expected to rely on will be ready could lead to unnecessary duplication of effort or difficulty in mitigating risks of their delayed completion. Indeed, the 2020 Census staff is already planning and carrying out activities in these areas. Although it is consulting with those responsible for the enterprise solutions, the Bureau's additionally producing a schedule for each of the enterprise solutions—including expected dates of delivery for tools, processes, and systems, such as 2020 Census is expected to use—would help minimize risks of developing decennial processes and tools incompatible with, or requiring time- or cost-intensive adjustment to harmonize with the forthcoming enterprise solutions.

Regarding the **involvement of stakeholders** in 2020 Census planning, according to senior Bureau officials, there has been little effective outreach by the Bureau to inform congressional staff about the scope of topics the Bureau has planned as part of its approach to fundamentally reexamine how it conducts a census. Bureau officials explained that their

---

[12]We are reviewing the Bureau's IT investment management processes and plan to issue a report later this year.

congressional outreach thus far has been on budgetary and non-decennial issues. We have previously reported on the importance of congressional outreach on the decennial to secure early agreement between the Bureau and Congress on the Bureau's fundamental approach for its next decennial.[13] Congressional support—regardless of the approach ultimately selected—is crucial for creating a stable environment in which to prepare for the census. Some of the Bureau's planned research, such as partial reliance on the Internet for data collection, has not been used by the Bureau on a large scale before, and the Director has also raised the possibility of a need for public debate on the trade-offs between census cost and census quality. Engaging in strategic bicameral and bipartisan communication can help build support for the Bureau's approach to fundamentally reexamine how it plans for and conducts a decennial census, and helps ensure an informed public debate on any potentially complex or sensitive topics.

The Bureau is piloting a process to **incorporate lessons learned** from recent oversight reporting and 2010 Census evaluations, and will need to take additional steps in order to rely on it as a mature tool to follow up on prior recommendations. We have previously reported that it will be vitally important for the Bureau to identify lessons learned from the 2010 Census to improve census-taking activities and address long-standing challenges.[14] The Bureau's process captures recommendations from recent 2010 Census evaluations and issues and assigns accountability for follow-up to staff working on research and testing, and the Bureau has plans to at least initially report on the status of recommendation follow-up. However, the Bureau lacks a formal process for periodically assessing the status of follow-up, and thus may lack consistent data to report and a basis for knowing when to hold staff accountable for that follow-up. The Bureau does not have in place a mechanism for systematic periodic reporting on the status of follow-up—such as on its intranet or Internet pages. Nor does it have performance measures defined for measuring the extent of recommendation follow-up, such as the percentage implemented or the percent not followed up on within 12 months, which would both allow the Bureau to more-easily track and report progress in incorporating improvements and begin to systematically incentivize team

---

[13]GAO, *2010 Census: Cost and Design Issues Need to be Addressed Soon*, GAO-04-37 (Washington, D.C.: Jan. 15, 2004).

[14]GAO-11-193.

or individual performance that incorporates lessons learned in order to help build a more results-oriented culture. Research and testing project teams reported out on which recommendations they would be addressing within their projects, as required by Bureau timelines, and described their plans for future action on recommendations. Taking these further steps will help sustain progress in ensuring the Bureau takes advantage of lessons from prior experiences and insights.

Bureau Is Incorporating Most Key Strategic Workforce Planning Practices but Does Not Yet Monitor Progress toward Workforce Goals

The Bureau is incorporating several key strategic workforce planning practices that address its objective of matching its managers, technical experts, and workforce to the demands of the 2020 Census. Strategic workforce planning encourages agency managers and stakeholders to systematically consider what is to be done, when and how it will be done, what skills will be needed, and how to gauge progress and results, helping to avoid staffing problems the Bureau has experienced in the past. For example, a Bureau assessment of its experience with 2010 Census observed that areas such as the management of large programs and projects, cost estimation, and sophisticated IT lacked staff with core skills and experience. Our prior work in human capital management has identified key practices in effective strategic workforce planning, five of which are:[15]

- identify current and future critical occupations, skills, and competencies and analyze workforce gaps,
- develop current and future strategies tailored to address gaps and human capital conditions in critical skills and competencies that need attention,
- involve top management, employees, and stakeholders in developing, communicating, and implementing the strategic workforce plan,
- align workforce planning with strategic planning and budget formulation, and
- monitor and evaluate progress toward achieving workforce planning and strategic goals.

---

[15]GAO, *Human Capital: Key Principles for Effective Strategic Workforce Planning*, GAO-04-39 (Washington, D.C.: Dec. 11, 2003) and *Workforce Planning: Interior, EPA, and the Forest Service Should Strengthen Linkages to Their Strategic Plans and Improve Evaluation*, GAO-10-413 (Washington, D.C.: Mar. 31, 2010). We combined a sixth leading practice, "build capacity to support workforce strategies," into these, to simplify presentation.

As figure 4 indicates, the Bureau is taking steps generally consistent with three of the five key strategic workforce planning leading practices for its planning of the 2020 Census, although the steps thus far are largely limited in scope to workforce planning for the second of the five 2020 Census phases—early research and testing. For example, the Bureau has begun to **identify current and future critical occupations** by piloting a skills and competency assessment of selected IT 2020 Census positions, including those for 2020 Census research and testing. In support of **developing current and future strategies tailored to address workforce gaps** that need attention, the Bureau has reviewed its available strategic hiring, retention, and other workforce flexibilities. In addition, **top management has been actively engaged** in communicating the strategic workforce plan, with the Bureau Director preparing staff for needed changes by speaking about it in town hall meetings and postings on his intranet blog.

Figure 4: Bureau Generally Relied on Key Leading Practices to Carry Out Workforce Planning for 2020 Census

Directions:

 Roll over each [Extent consistent] bar to see more information regarding illustrative steps taken and illustrative steps remaining that contributed to the rating given.

Identify current and future critical occupations, skills, and competencies and analyze workforce gaps

Identify mission-critical occupations and competencies, which form the basis for much of workforce planning.

Generally consistent

Develop current and future strategies tailored to address gaps and human capital conditions in critical skills and competencies that need attention

Develop reasonable human capital strategies and tools and align these to eliminate gaps and improve the contribution of critical skills and competencies.

Generally consistent

Monitor and evaluate progress toward achieving workforce planning and strategic goals

Assess progress to determine whether workforce planning goals are being met and identify the reasons for any shortfalls.

Not consistent

Involve top management, employees, and other stakeholders in developing, communicating, and implementing the strategic workforce plan

Involve top management, employees and stakeholders in unique roles to design strategic workforce plans.

Partially consistent

Align workforce planning with strategic planning and budget formulation

Align workforce and strategic plans with budget.

Generally consistent

Source: GAO analysis of U.S. Census Bureau information.

Notes:

Illustrative steps taken to date: GAO assessments based on Bureau steps taken as of April 10, 2012.

Extent consistent: We determined that steps taken or planned were either *"generally," "partially," or "not"* consistent with respective practices.

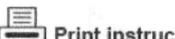 **Print instructions** | To print text version of this graphic, go to appendix IV.

Figure 4 also shows that the Bureau plans to take a number of steps over the next few months that are generally consistent with the key strategic workforce planning leading practices. For example, in support of the practice to **analyze workforce gaps** the Bureau plans to finalize in May its project plan detailing the steps, resources, and timeline for conducting its Bureau-wide skills gap and competency assessment that it will undertake later in 2012. To help **develop current and future strategies**, in June, the Bureau plans to identify which of its existing training courses can potentially help address gaps it expects it may identify, while in August, it plans to document how its skills gap and competency analyses will be updated and used during later census phases with target time-windows for later activity, including how it will **align with budget formulation**. The Bureau planned some of these steps in response to our discussions with its workforce planning officials.

The Bureau's early effort to analyze competencies has the potential to help it **identify critical occupations and skills** that will help it adjust to changes in technology, budget constraints, and other factors that alter the environment in which it operates. **Top management is actively engaged** in developing the workforce plan and is setting the overall direction for planning efforts. The Bureau's plan to document when skills gap and competency analyses will be conducted for future 2020 Census phases will help the Bureau manage other supporting activity to ensure that this important workforce planning activity happens soon.

Still, the Bureau could do more to implement its strategic workforce planning consistent with key leading practices. The Bureau has not yet **determined its workforce goals** from its skills gap and competency analyses or laid out how it will monitor, report, and evaluate progress in achieving them. According to the Bureau, it hopes to enable program managers to flexibly, and on-demand, obtain reports on the status and strategies targeted to their own goals and workforce needs. Identifying agency goals for this initiative and a vital few performance measures can help agency officials think through the scope, timing, and possible barriers to evaluating and implementing the resulting workforce plans, and the monitoring and evaluation itself can provide information for effective oversight by identifying performance shortfalls and appropriate corrective actions.

Finally, the Bureau has traditionally obtained input on decennial technical, operational, and policy issues from a diverse group of stakeholders, but, according to Bureau officials, has not yet considered the **role of external stakeholders** in developing, communicating, and implementing its workforce planning. External stakeholders with appropriate expertise and experience can play a useful role in supporting an agency with its workforce planning such as by serving as a sounding board for agency workforce initiatives. For example, academic institutions and their accreditation organizations are positioned to discuss both the direction the respective academic programs are headed and whether agency needs can be expected to be met by them. A panel of academics from universities with relevant expertise might provide a two-way forum for how to align future skills and competency needs for the agency workforce with the hiring pool that the academic institutions are helping to develop. Expanding discussions with traditional census advisory groups, such as those organized to tap professional organizations and diversity perspectives, may also provide insights and advice on recruiting, retaining, and developing staff. Identifying those external stakeholders who can provide insights to Bureau workforce planning challenges and reaching out to them could help the Bureau develop strategies to help meet its objective of having a workforce matched with the demands of the 2020 Census.

Conclusions

The Bureau faces many challenges—internally and externally—in preparing for a cost-effective 2020 Census, including transforming the Bureau's internal organization; rethinking the way the Bureau plans for and executes decennial censuses; and assessing the skills and competencies of the Bureau's workforce. Applying leading management practices in each of these areas of the Bureau's preparation for the 2020 Census can help ensure that the Bureau addresses these challenges and delivers high-quality and timely results. Other areas of planning, such as IT investment management, that are outside the scope of our review will also require sustained attention. However, sustaining these efforts going forward, especially given the Director's pending August 2012 departure and the Bureau's historic issue of leadership continuity, will be a challenge.

The Bureau is generally or partially following most leading practices in the management areas of organizational transformation, long-term project planning, and strategic workforce planning—positioning itself well during this early phase of planning for the 2020 Census. Much of the Bureau's early progress is visible in its plans for additional activity over the coming months; equally important will be the need to finalize these plans and execute these activities in a timely manner to maintain the Bureau's early momentum toward a cost-effective 2020 Census.

It will be important for the Bureau to take additional steps to further implement leading practices in each of the three management areas we reviewed. Reexamining its planned transformation activities in terms of resources allocated to them will help ensure that its **organizational transformation** team can prioritize and implement those activities, properly use supporting data to enhance those activities, or identify and mitigate risks to their implementation. The Bureau's **long-term planning** will be aided by improvements in scheduling that will help to ensure the coordination, management, and resource allocation to activities as needed, and by a congressional outreach strategy that helps ensure stakeholders are informed of new census design elements and possible cost-quality trade-offs. In addition, improvements in the assessment and reporting on the Bureau's recommendation follow-up system will help the Bureau get the best return on that investment. Finally, for **strategic workforce planning**, it will be important that the Bureau set agency workforce goals so that it can determine how to monitor, report, and evaluate its progress toward achieving those goals. Moving forward, identifying external stakeholders with expertise and experience in workforce planning challenges such as recruitment and soliciting feedback from them will help the Bureau develop strategies to meet its objective of having a workforce matched with the demands of the 2020 Census. Implementing these remaining leading practices can help the Bureau stay on track for a well-planned, well-executed 2020 Census.

Recommendations for Executive Action

We recommend that the Secretary of Commerce require the Under Secretary for Economic Affairs who oversees the Economics and Statistics Administration, as well as the Director of the U.S. Census Bureau, to take the following six actions to improve the Bureau's process of organizational transformation, long-term planning, and strategic workforce planning for the 2020 Census, and thus better position the Bureau to carry out a cost-effective decennial census:

Organizational Transformation

1. In order to ensure the Bureau's decennial organizational transformation is sustained and successful, examine the alignment between the levels of activity planned for the transformation and the resources dedicated to their implementation, and adjust the activity and resources as appropriate.

Long-term Planning

2. In order to ensure prioritization and timely completion of all necessary research and testing efforts, as well as timely transition to later 2020 Census phases, develop and implement a long-term planning schedule that includes key milestones and deadlines, including
   - deadlines for decisions that directly affect activity in later 2020 Census phases;
   - a schedule for creating, revising, or updating governance, program management, and system engineering and architecture plans to be used in later 2020 Census phases beyond research and testing; and
   - expected times of delivery for Bureau-wide enterprise tools, processes, and standards that 2020 Census planning would be expected to use.

3. In order to inform congressional decision-making related to the 2020 Census, develop and implement an effective congressional outreach strategy, particularly on new design elements the Bureau is researching and considering as well as on cost-quality trade-offs of potential design decisions.

4. In order to improve the Bureau's process for following up on Bureau and oversight agencies' recommendations to improve the 2020 Census,
   - assess the status of recommendation follow-up at regular intervals, such as every 12 months; and
   - periodically report on the status of recommendation follow-up— such as on the Bureau's intranet or Internet pages

Strategic Workforce Planning

5. In order to help the Bureau identify performance shortfalls and appropriate corrective actions in achieving its strategic workforce planning goals, set agency workforce planning goals, and determine how the Bureau will monitor, report, and evaluate its progress toward achieving those goals.

6. In order to help the Bureau develop strategies to meet its objective of having a workforce matched with the demands of the 2020 Census, identify external stakeholders whose expertise and experience can provide insights to Bureau workforce planning challenges, such as recruitment, and reach out to them and incorporate their input as appropriate.

Agency Comments and Our Evaluation

We provided a draft of this report to the Secretary of Commerce on April 26, 2012 and received the department's written comments on May 11, 2012. The comments are reprinted in appendix VI. The Department of Commerce concurred with our findings and recommendations.

In its comments, the department provided additional context on the role that the Bureau's Human Resources Division plays handling strategic workforce planning for the 2020 Census. We have included this additional information in the background section of the report where we first discuss the assessment and analysis initiative.

Also, the department noted that after it had received our draft report, the Bureau had added additional staff and contractor support to its organizational transformation activities. We have included this additional information in the report where we discuss the organizational transformation leading practices. The Bureau's action appears responsive to our recommendation, and we will further assess this as part of our routine recommendation follow-up process.

We are sending copies of this report to the Secretary of Commerce, the Director of the U.S. Census Bureau, and interested congressional committees. The report also is available at no charge on GAO's website at http://www.gao.gov.

If you have any questions about this report please contact me at (202) 512-2757 or goldenkoffr@gao.gov. Contact points for our Offices of Congressional Relations and Public Affairs may be found on the last page of this report. The GAO staff that made key contributions to this report is listed in appendix VII.

Robert Goldenkoff
Director
Strategic Issues

The Honorable Thomas R. Carper
Chairman
The Honorable Scott Brown
Ranking Member
Subcommittee on Federal Financial Management, Government
  Information, Federal Services, and International Security
Committee on Homeland Security and Governmental Affairs
United States Senate

The Honorable Danny K. Davis
Ranking Member
Subcommittee on Health Care, District of Columbia, Census,
  and the National Archives
Committee on Oversight and Government Reform
House of Representatives

Appendix I: Objectives, Scope, and Methodology

The objectives of our review were to assess the extent to which the U.S. Census Bureau's (Bureau) 2020 Directorate and its Research and Planning Office are taking steps consistent with leading practices for organizational transformation, long-term project planning, and strategic workforce planning. For each of these three management areas, we conducted a literature review to develop the appropriate leading practices that should be considered in our review.

We identified leading practices from the following sources:

- Organizational Transformation: Our prior report for federal agencies to consider as they seek to transform their culture in response to governance challenges.[1]
- Long-term project planning: Our evaluation of the Bureau's early project-planning efforts of the 2010 Census[2] and information from the Software Engineering Institute.[3]
- Strategic workforce planning: Our two prior reports[4] that developed the practices, and on selected material from the GAO Management Diagnostic Tool,[5] the Project Management Institute,[6] and the Office of

---

[1]GAO, *Results-Oriented Cultures: Implementation Steps to Assist Mergers and Organizational Transformations* (GAO-03-669) (Washington, D.C.: July 2, 2003). Not all of the leading practices from this report were used because some were not germane to the Bureau.

[2]GAO, *2010 Census: Cost and Design Issues Need to Be Addressed Soon*, GAO-04-37 (Washington, D.C.: Jan, 15, 2004).

[3]Carnegie Mellon University's Software Engineering Institute (SEI), recognized for its expertise in software processes, has developed models and methods that define and determine organizations' software process maturity and has been used by GAO in the past to develop leading practices.

[4]GAO, *Human Capital: Key Principles for Effective Strategic Workforce Planning*, GAO-04-39 (Washington, D.C.: Dec. 11, 2003) and *Workforce Planning: Interior, EPA, and the Forest Service Should Strengthen Linkages to Their Strategic Plans and Improve Evaluation*, GAO-10-413 (Washington, D.C.: Mar. 31, 2010).

[5]GAO developed the Management Diagnostic Survey as a tool that could be used by executive agencies and GAO to identify management function areas in which an agency is performing well or may have opportunity to better implement leading management practices. The result can assist GAO to determine areas for additional follow-up work and can help agency leaders identify management improvement opportunities. From this tool, we used information pertaining to human capital.

[6]The Project Management Institute purpose is to advance the project-management profession through standards and certifications, collaborative communities, research, and professional-development opportunities.

Personnel Management's Human Capital Assessment and
Accountability Framework (HCAAF).[7]

To assess the extent to which the Bureau implemented the practices, we
reviewed numerous Bureau documents pertaining to the early planning of
the 2020 Census. These generally consisted of high-level strategic
framework documents, strategies and plans pertaining to specific
elements of the 2020 Census, planning memorandums, charters for key
steering groups, and timelines for execution. Many of these documents
were considered draft, but Bureau officials said were sufficiently
developed for purposes of our review. We accessed the Bureau's intranet
to see what information it provides employees about the topics of our
research objectives. We also obtained performance contracts of Senior
Executive Service officials to evaluate the extent to which performance
expectations include 2020 Census planning goals.

We interviewed Bureau officials responsible for the early planning of the
2020 Census, including: the Bureau Director; the 2020 Directorate's
Research and Planning Office; the Associate Director for
Communications; and senior officials in the Human Resource Division.
We also met with members of the 2020 Census Directorate's
Organizational Change Management Council, which is charged with
effectively managing the delivery of the new organization design and
providing executive guidance, support, and resolution of the
transformation.

From our review of documents and interviews with all agency officials, we
determined the extent to which each leading practice has been
implemented using a scale of "generally consistent," "partially consistent,"
and "not consistent." A practice was considered "generally consistent"
when the evidence demonstrated the Bureau generally fulfilled more than
half the description of the practice. A practice was considered "partially
consistent" when the evidence demonstrated some meaningful actions
had been taken, but less than half the description of the practice was
fulfilled. A practice was considered "not consistent" when the evidence
indicated the practice was not addressed because either no action was
yet taken or the actions that were taken were minimal or not effective.

---

[7]The Office of Personnel Management's HCAAF, developed in conjunction with the Office
of Management and Budget and GAO, defines standards for success for the federal
government and can serve as a road map for human capital transformation.

We reached our assessments by having the primary team members
determine their collective opinion and then sought validation by having
another GAO subject-matter specialist with sufficient familiarity with the
material use professional judgment and develop an independent
assessment. In all circumstances, the coders collaborated to discuss any
differences, which resulted in developing a consensus assessment.

Appendix II: Bureau Is Using Selected Key Practices to Carry Out Organizational Transformation for 2020 Census Directorate (Text for Interactive Fig. 2)

Key practice	Description	Illustrative steps taken to date[a]	Illustrative steps planned (expected date)	Extent steps are consistent with practice[b]
Ensure top leadership drives the transformation.	• Define and articulate a compelling reason for change. • Document rationale, expected benefits, and definition of success.	• Issued strategic plan for 2020 Census with annual updates of a business plan. • Included rationale, benefits, and description of factors that will contribute to success in strategy documents. • Chartered an organizational change management council comprising Bureau-wide executives and senior managers.	• Identify indicators of success (May 2012).	Generally consistent
Focus on a key set of principles and priorities at the outset of the transformation.	• Embed core values in every aspect of the organization to reinforce the new culture.	• Created change management strategy documents explicitly referring to 2020 Census goals and guiding principles. • Established eight guiding principles for the transformation.	• Incorporate key principles for the transformation in planned activity for interacting with staff (July 2012).	Generally consistent
Set implementation goals and a timeline to build momentum and show progress.	• Make public implementation goals and timeline. • Monitor employee attitudes and take appropriate action.	• Created high-level transformation timeline that includes milestones for governance, communication and education, and transition activities. • Created draft strategy documents that include targets for achieving "quick wins," periodic reporting, and outreach events to build momentum.	• Identify measures for monitoring progress of transformation (May 2012). • Begin public dissemination of goals and timelines (July 2012). • Finalize comprehensive plan for engaging staff and stakeholders in determining what the new organization should be (June 2012). • Finalize transition timeline subject to approval of proposed changes (February 2013).	Generally consistent

Key practice	Description	Illustrative steps taken to date[a]	Illustrative steps planned (expected date)	Extent steps are consistent with practice[b]
Dedicate an implementation team to manage the transformation process.	• Establish networks to support implementation team. • Select high-performing team members.	• Designated an "organizational change manager" responsible for day-to-day organizational change activities.	• Include expectations within performance plans of senior managers below executive level to support transformation (October 2012).	Partially consistent **Additional Step Needed** Examine sufficiency of resources of implementation team.
Involve employees to obtain their ideas and gain their ownership for the transformation.	• Use employee teams. • Incorporate employee feedback. • Delegate authority to appropriate organizational levels.	• Created a transformation plan that specifies a series of workshops, focus groups, and other employee-centered processes.	• Convene and enlist support of a group of managers across every affected division and branch (May 2012). • Convene town hall meetings to roll out strategy to employees (June 2012). • Implement a vehicle to obtain anonymous employee ideas and feedback on proposals (June 2012). • Begin series of workshops and focus groups (July 2012). • Make details available to staff on specific changes to be made (February 2013).	Generally consistent
Establish a communication strategy to create shared expectations and report related progress.	• Communicate early and often. • Ensure message consistency. • Encourage two-way communication. • Provide information to meet employee needs.	• Discussed vision for transformation at unit staff meetings, fielding questions and comments. • Created communication team to support organizational change management.	• Develop comprehensive communication strategy (May 2012). • Create and maintain an intranet site to provide an official clearing house of information, answers to frequently asked questions, and points of contact for all staff (June 2012). • Communicate details about specific future changes being planned (February 2013).	Generally consistent

Source: GAO analysis of U.S. Census Bureau information.

[a]As of April 10, 2012.

[b]We determined that steps taken or planned were either "generally," "partially," or "not" consistent with respective practices.

Key practice	Description	Illustrative steps taken to date[a]	Illustrative steps planned (expected date)	Extent steps are consistent with practice[b]
Develop a project plan.	Consider all phases of the project and have clear and measurable goals; clearly state all assumptions, schedules, and deadlines; and identify needed skills and resources.	• In a series of eight memos, laid out a framework documenting goals, assumptions, and timing of five broad phases for 2020 Census with cost estimate milestones tied to annual budget request submissions. • Maintained high-level schedule of activities for remaining four phases. • Documented initial work requirements and interdependencies for all fiscal year 2012 research and testing projects.	• Finalize detailed schedule of all program management, systems engineering, requirements, and training activities (August 2012). • Finalize project plans for all research and testing projects begun in fiscal year 2012 (August 2012). • Update program management and systems engineering training materials to reflect finalized processes (September 2012).	Partially consistent **Additional steps needed** • Document deadlines and decisions affecting later phases of 2020 Census. • Document schedule for updating or replacing current management documents for later phases of 2020 Census. • Document timeline for delivering Bureau-wide enterprise solutions.
Involve stakeholders.	• Involve internal and external stakeholders in the decision-making process. • Focus on the highest priority stakeholder needs and mission goals.	• Conducted 14 planning workshops with internal and external stakeholders to identify design options to explore. • Presented high-level description of research plans for selected technical areas to scientific and data user advisory groups. • Rechartered race and ethnicity advisory committees.	• Finalize communications plan for informing and soliciting feedback from staff and stakeholders (September 2012).	Partially consistent **Additional step needed** • Develop a plan for effective outreach to congress, specifically on sensitive research and design issues such as privacy and cost-quality trade-offs.

Key practice	Description	Illustrative steps taken to date[a]	Illustrative steps planned (expected date)	Extent steps are consistent with practice[b]
Incorporate lessons learned.	• Evaluate past performance and capitalize on lessons learned to improve performance. • Includes the processes required to use project information to improve future efforts.	• Sought to avoid prior census planning problems, such as unreliable cost estimates, fragmented and late planning, and not relying on evidence from such sources as research and testing. • Involved former Bureau executives in planning workshops. • Implemented a database for tracking action plans and status of prior recommendations.	• Complete 2010 evaluations critical for early research and testing (September 2012).	Partially consistent **Additional step needed** • Recommendation follow-up process requires additional steps to ensure follow-up on prior recommendations.
Analyze and mitigate risks.	• Identify, analyze, prioritize, and document risks. Ideally, assess more than one alternative. • Plan risk management— the process of defining how to conduct risk management activities for a project.	• Featured analyses of risks prominently in early planning activity. • Created 2020 Census research and testing risk register, and included risk in regular executive discussions. • Risk management documents were among the first to be finalized.	• Adjust 2020 Census risk management processes to align with separate Bureau-wide processes being developed (August 2012).	Generally consistent
Monitor progress.	• Identify measurable performance goals that describe and guide successful planning. Collect performance data and report it to determine how well the goals are being achieved.	• Ensured that individual research projects describe their own performance measures.	• Begin issuing monthly status reports at the program level (May 2012).	Generally consistent

Source: GAO analysis of U.S. Census Bureau information.

[a]As of April 10, 2012.

[b]We determined that steps taken or planned were either "generally," "partially," or "not" consistent with respective practices.

Appendix IV: Bureau Generally Relied on Key Leading Practices to Carry Out Workforce Planning for 2020 Census (Text for Interactive Fig. 4)

Key practice	Description	Illustrative steps taken to date[a]	Illustrative steps planned (expected date)	Extent steps are consistent with practice[b]
Identify current and future critical occupations, skills, and competencies and analyze workforce gaps.	• Identify mission-critical occupations and competencies, which form the basis for much of workforce planning.	• Piloted skills and competency assessment of selected IT positions including those for the second of five 2020 Census phases.	• Finalize project plan detailing the steps, resources, and timeline for conducting Bureau-wide skills gap assessment (May 2012). • Validate competency dictionary with subject-matter experts throughout Bureau (May 2012). • Begin Bureau-wide skills gap and competency assessment (September 2012). • Research and testing project teams finalize list of needed skills (August 2012).	Generally consistent
Develop current and future strategies tailored to address gaps and human capital conditions in critical skills and competencies that need attention.	• Develop reasonable human capital strategies and tools and align these to eliminate gaps and improve the contribution of critical skills and competencies.	• Inventoried available strategic flexibilities.	• Finalize project plan detailing the steps, resources, and timeline for conducting Bureau-wide skills gap assessment (May 2012). • Identify existing training courses within Bureau to potentially address gaps (June 2012).	Generally consistent

Key practice	Description	Illustrative steps taken to date[a]	Illustrative steps planned (expected date)	Extent steps are consistent with practice[b]
Monitor and evaluate progress toward achieving workforce planning and strategic goals.	• Assess progress to determine whether workforce planning goals are being met and identify the reasons for any shortfalls.			Not consistent **Missing steps needed** • Develop process and specific goals for monitoring, reporting, and evaluating Bureau's progress toward workforce goals. • Begin reporting on Bureau's progress toward workforce goals.
Involve top management, employees, and other stakeholders in developing, communicating, and implementing the strategic workforce plan.	• Involve top management, employees and stakeholders in unique active roles to design strategic workforce plans.	• Director spoke internally and externally about need for workforce analyses to align with future strategies. • Bureau meets monthly with departmental officials on human capital initiatives. • Bureau offered specific professional development courses on the basis of recommendation of human capital team.	• Rely on employee focus groups to validate competencies (May 2012). • Begin communicating to entire staff about skills gap analyses. (June 2012).	Partially consistent **Missing step needed** • Identify external stakeholders and begin outreach on workforce planning efforts.
Align workforce planning with strategic planning and budget formulation.	• Align workforce and strategic plans with budget.	• Human capital management plan requires inputs from budget and alignment with strategic plans.	• Document how skills gap and competency analyses will be updated and how it will be used during later phases, including target time windows for later activity (August 2012).	Generally consistent

Source: GAO analysis of U.S. Census Bureau information.

[a]As of April 10, 2012.

[b]We determined that steps taken or planned were either "generally," "partially," or "not" consistent with respective practices.

Appendix V: List of the U.S. Census Bureau's Program Management Planning Documents

Consistent with the leading practices of developing a project plan, and to help operationalize its high-level plan, the U.S. Census Bureau (Bureau) has identified 19 specific management process areas from management literature for executing and controlling its research and testing projects for 2020 Census (see table 1). For many of these areas the Bureau has developed a management-strategy paper that typically includes standardized sections addressing links to strategic goals, performance measures, objectives, and strategies; standards and guidelines; roles and responsibilities; and key assumptions and risks. The Bureau is following up on each of these strategies with a more-detailed management-planning document that identifies specific methods and techniques the Bureau will use to implement the strategy as well as how the actions will link to the Bureau's other broader strategic documents. In some areas, the Bureau is bypassing the strategy paper and has either produced or is planning to produce a finalized—or what the Bureau refers to as a "baselined"—plan.

Table 1: Bureau's Program Management Planning Documents

Program management area	Strategy issued[a]	Plan formalized (or estimated date)[a]
Risk Management	May 2011	August 2011
Strategic Plan	[b]	September 2010
Acquisition and Sourcing	June 2011	Fiscal year 2012 Q4
Budget Management Process	May 2011	Fiscal year2012 Q4
Communication and Stakeholder Engagement	November 2011	Fiscal year 2012 Q4
Document Management	[c]	Fiscal year 2012 Q3
Earned Value Management Implementation	[d]	[d]
Governance	October 2011	Fiscal year 2012 Q4
Human Capital Management	November 2011	Fiscal year 2012 Q4
Integrated Program Control & Performance Measurement	June 2011	Fiscal year 2012 Q4
Issue Management	May 2011	Fiscal year 2012 Q4
Knowledge Management	May 2011	Fiscal year 2012 Q4
Performance Management	June 2011	Fiscal year 2012 Q4
Process Quality Assurance Management	Fiscal year 2012 Q3	Fiscal year 2012 Q4
Program Change Control Management	May 2011	Fiscal year 2012 Q4
Requirements Engineering	September 2011	Fiscal year 2012 Q4
Research and Testing	November 2011	Fiscal year 2012 Q4

Program management area	Strategy issued[a]	Plan formalized (or estimated date)[a]
Schedule Management	May 2011	Fiscal year 2012 Q4
Training (2012-2014)	[c]	Fiscal year 2012 Q4

Source: GAO analysis of U.S. Census Bureau data.

[a]Status as of April 10, 2012

[b]No separate strategy document was developed for the 2020 Census Strategic Plan.

[c]The Bureau is skipping the production of some strategies and simply issuing plans.

[d]2020 Census staff awaits resolution of Bureau-wide strategy and guidance before attempting to develop decennial-specific plans for using earned value management.

Appendix VI: Comments from the Department of Commerce

Note: Page and paragraph numbers in the draft report may differ from those in this report.

UNITED STATES DEPARTMENT OF COMMERCE
The Secretary of Commerce
Washington, D.C. 20230

May 11, 2012

Mr. Robert Goldenkoff
Director, Strategic Issues
U.S. Government Accountability Office
Washington, DC 20548

Dear Mr. Goldenkoff:

The U.S. Department of Commerce appreciates the opportunity to comment on the U.S. Government Accountability Office's draft report, *2020 Census - Additional Steps Are Needed to Build on Early Planning* (GAO-12-626). The Department's comments on this report are enclosed.

Sincerely,

John E. Bryson

Enclosure

GAO Draft Report
2020 Census: Additional Steps Are Needed to Build on Early Planning
U.S. Census Bureau Response

The U.S. Census Bureau at the Department of Commerce would like to thank the Government Accountability Office (GAO) for its assessment of additional steps needed to improve early planning for the 2020 Census. We appreciate the opportunity to review and comment on this draft report, and we concur with GAO's findings. We look forward to providing an action plan to address GAO's recommendations.

We have no significant comments or concerns about the facts of the report with two exceptions. While the 2020 Directorate and the 2020 Research and Planning office are engaged in efforts consistent with "leading practices for organizational transformation" as well as "long-term project planning," our Human Resources Division, in collaboration with the 2020 Directorate, is handling "strategic workforce planning for the 2020 Census" (page 2, 3rd paragraph). We think that it would be helpful if GAO clarified these responsibilities. In addition, the report mentions that all of the work associated with the organizational changes the 2020 Directorate has embarked upon "seem to be substantial work for the sole staff member dedicated at this time to transformation" (page 8). Since this draft report was issued additional staff have been placed on the project and Mitre Corporation is now supporting these efforts as well.

With the exception of this minor clarification, GAO's observations and recommendations are consistent with those held by the leadership of the 2020 program. Improvements are already under way to strengthen the program in the areas GAO has identified.

Appendix VII: GAO Contact and Staff Acknowledgments

GAO Contact	Robert Goldenkoff, (202) 512-2757 or goldenkoffr@gao.gov
Staff Acknowledgments	In addition to the contact named above, Ty Mitchell, Assistant Director; James Cook; Elizabeth Curda; Jeff Demarco; Vijay D'Souza; Ron Fecso; Geoff King; Andrea Levine; Steven Lozano; Signora May; Donna Miller; Janice Morrison; Melanie Papasian; Lisa Pearson; Cynthia Saunders; and Sarah Veale made key contributions to this report.

Related GAO Products

Decennial Census: Additional Actions Could Improve the Census Bureau's Ability to Control Costs for the 2020 Census. GAO-12-80. Washington, D.C.: January 24, 2012.

2010 Census: Preliminary Lessons Learned Highlight the Need for Fundamental Reforms. GAO-11-496T. Washington, D.C., April 6, 2011.

2010 Census: Data Collection Operations Were Generally Completed as Planned, but Long-standing Challenges Suggest Need for Fundamental Reforms. GAO-11-193. Washington, D.C.: December 14, 2010.

Workforce Planning: Interior, EPA, and the Forest Service Should Strengthen Linkages to Their Strategic Plans and Improve Evaluation. GAO-10-413. Washington, D.C.: March 31, 2010.

Information Technology: Significant Problems of Critical Automation Program Contribute to Risks Facing 2010 Census. GAO-08-550T. Washington, D.C.: March 5, 2008.

2010 Census: Cost and Design Issues Need to Be Addressed Soon. GAO-04-37. Washington, D.C.: January 15, 2004.

Human Capital: Key Principles for Effective Strategic Workforce Planning. GAO-04-39. Washington, D.C.: December 11, 2003.

Results-Oriented Cultures: Implementation Steps to Assist Mergers and Organizational Transformations. GAO-03-669. Washington, D.C.: July 2, 2003.

High-Risk Series: Quick Reference Guide. GAO/HR-97-2. Washington, D.C.: February 1997.

www.ingramcontent.com/pod-product-compliance
Lightning Source LLC
Chambersburg PA
CBHW080921290526
45795CB00007BA/2603